A HOW-TO FOR BEGINNERS

lettering FOR THE Lord

DRILLS, PROJECTS & PRACTICE!

TABLE OF CONTENTS

.... let's begin...

introduction

Hi, friends! This book is jam packed with lettering goodies to get you started on your lettering journey! You'll find tips, tricks, and loads of alphabets and practice pages to help you master this new skill! The most important part of this journey is truly practice, practice, practice! As you memorize each stroke, your muscles will commit each letter to memory and that is when the fun begins. Once you have mastered your letter drills, you can begin to really create custom lettering art. So use all the space provided to you for practice in this book and you can also buy tracing paper and layer it over the pages of this book for additional practice tracing over letters and words! This book is also filled with love for the Lord! May these words and this beautiful new skill bless you and provide you with peace from above!

LETTERING BASICS

Let's get started by going over some lettering basics!

SCRIPT   This lettering style mimics calligraphy or cursive. It is a favorite among many because of the flow and beauty of each stroke!

SERIF

SERIF   This alphabet style is popular because it is the easiest to read. Serifs are the small strokes added to the end of each main lettering stroke.

SANS SERIF

SANS SERIF   This lettering style can be very playful and add a nice contrast to the elegant flow of script! You'll see that this lettering style is similar to the serif but without the small strokes on the top and bottom. The word "sans" means without in French, so this style is without serifs!

6

TOOLS

The beauty of hand lettering is that you really only need pencil and paper to begin! However, you can spice it up by using a few different mediums we'll discuss below!

PENCILS

The easiest tool! Grab a mechanical pencil and you can letter anywhere!

PENS

Micron Pens come in a variety of sizes and are great, high quality lettering pens. Sharpies are also a fun medium to try!

COLORED PENCILS

Try Prismacolor Pencils to add depth and a pop of color!

MARKERS

Whether you buy Crayolas or a nice set of alcohol markers, this medium can provide beautiful results!

WATERCOLOR

Once you've mastered pen and pencil, watercolors provide an amazing new challenge for your lettering journey!

CHALK

If you love the look of black and white lettering art then chalk may be your new favorite medium! Chalk gives you the opportunity to use the chalk dust to create depth & shadows!

LETTER DRILLS

LOWERCASE SCRIPT ALPHABET

a b c d e f g

h i j k l m n

o p q r s t u

v w x y z

ON THE FOLLOWING PAGE YOU WILL BEGIN LETTER DRILLS
FOR THIS LOWERCASE SCRIPT ALPHABET! REMEMBER THAT
LETTER DRILLS ARE THE BASE FOR MASTERING HAND
LETTERING SO THERE IS EXTRA SPACE TO PRACTICE,
PRACTICE, PRACTICE! LET'S BEGIN...

a a a

b b b

c c c

d d d

e e e

f f f

g g g

h h h

i   *i*   *i*

j   *j*   *j*

k   *k*   *k*

l   *l*   *l*

m   *m*   *m*

n   *n*   *n*

o   *o*   *o*

p   *p*   *p*

q   q   q

r   r   r

s   s   s

t   t   t

u   u   u

v   v   v

w   w   w

x   x   x

y y y

z z z

UPPERCASE SCRIPT ALPHABET

ON THE FOLLOWING PAGE YOU WILL BEGIN LETTER DRILLS FOR THIS UPPERCASE SCRIPT ALPHABET. AS WITH THE FIRST SET OF LETTER DRILLS, THERE IS EXTRA SPACE TO PRACTICE. DEVELOPING THAT MUSCLE MEMORY WILL BE KEY WHEN YOU START TO WRITE WORDS! LET'S GET STARTED...

$\mathcal{Y}$ $\mathcal{Y}$ $\mathcal{Y}$

$\mathcal{Z}$ $\mathcal{Z}$ $\mathcal{Z}$

A B C D E F G

H I J K L M N

O P Q R S T U

V W X Y Z

THIS IS AN EXAMPLE OF A SANS SERIF ALPHABET. THIS IS THE PERFECT STYLE TO MIX AND MATCH WITH YOUR SCRIPT LETTERS. WHILE THIS ALPHABET MAY LOOK EASIER TO WRITE, IT STILL TAKES PRACTICE AND MUSCLE MEMORY TO MASTER! LET'S GET PRACTICING...

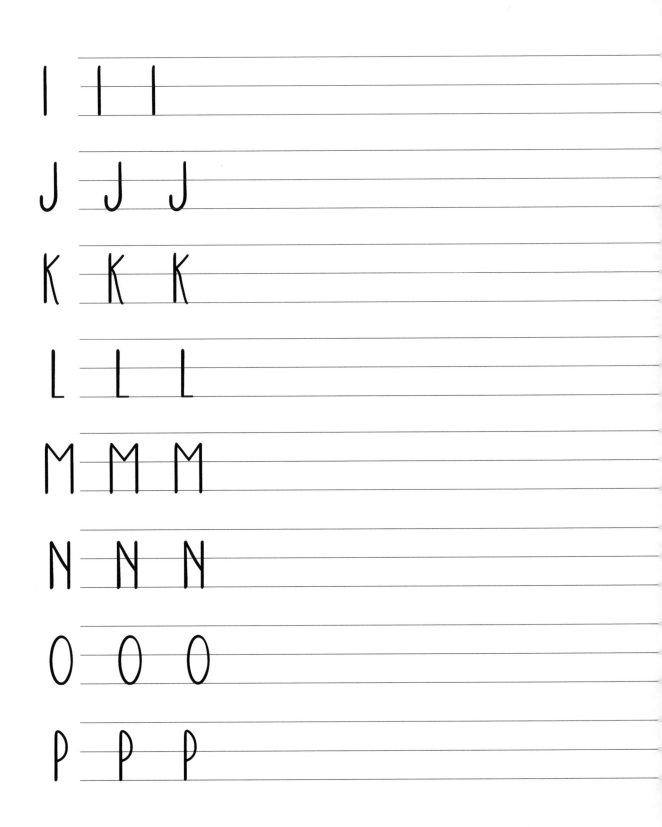

I I I

J J J

K K K

L L L

M M M

N N N

O O O

P P P

Q Q Q

R R R

S S S

T T T

U U U

V V V

W W W

X X X

Y Y Y

Z Z Z

A B C D E F G

H I J K L M N

O P Q R S T U

V W X Y Z

THIS IS AN EXAMPLE OF A SERIF ALPHABET. THIS IS ANOTHER
FUN STYLE TO MIX WITH YOUR SCRIPT ALPHABET LETTERS.
THIS ALPHABET REQUIRES YOU TO FILL IN THE DOWNSTROKES
AS WELL AS ADD THE SERIF TO THE TOP AND BOTTOM OF
EACH LETTER. LET'S START PRACTICING...

A A A

B B B

C C C

D D D

E E E

F F F

G G G

H H H

I I I

J J J

K K K

L L L

M M M

N N N

O O O

P P P

Q Q Q

R R R

S S S

T T T

U U U

V V V

W W W

X X X

Y Y Y

Z Z Z

PRACTICE WORDS & PROJECTS

PRACTICE WORD:

believe

TRACE:

believe

PRACTICE:

42

PRACTICE WORD:

TRACE:

PRACTICE:

PRACTICE WORD:

hope

TRACE:

PRACTICE:

PRACTICE WORD:

TRACE:

love

PRACTICE:

PRACTICE WORD:

TRACE:

PRACTICE:

PRACTICE WORD:

TRACE:

PRACTICE:

prayer

TRACE:

prayer

PRACTICE:

PRACTICE WORD:

grace

TRACE:

grace

PRACTICE:

PRACTICE WORD:

disciple

TRACE:

disciple

PRACTICE:

PRACTICE WORD:

TRACE:

PRACTICE:

PRACTICE WORD:

heaven

TRACE:

heaven

PRACTICE:

PRACTICE WORD:

wisdom

TRACE:

wisdom

PRACTICE:

PRACTICE WORD:

bible

TRACE:

bible

PRACTICE:

PRACTICE WORD:

peace

TRACE:

peace

PRACTICE:

PRACTICE WORD:

scripture

TRACE:

scripture

PRACTICE:

PRACTICE WORD:

joyful

TRACE:

joyful

PRACTICE:

PRACTICE WORD:

righteous

TRACE:

righteous

PRACTICE:

PRACTICE WORD:

mercy

TRACE:

mercy

PRACTICE:

PRACTICE WORD:

praise

TRACE:

praise

PRACTICE:

PRACTICE WORD:

hallelujah

TRACE:

hallelujah

PRACTICE:

amen

TRACE:

amen

PRACTICE:

PRACTICE WORD:

blessed

TRACE:

blessed

PRACTICE:

PROJECT 1:

PRACTICE:

take heart

JOHN 16:33

PRACTICE:

PROJECT 3:

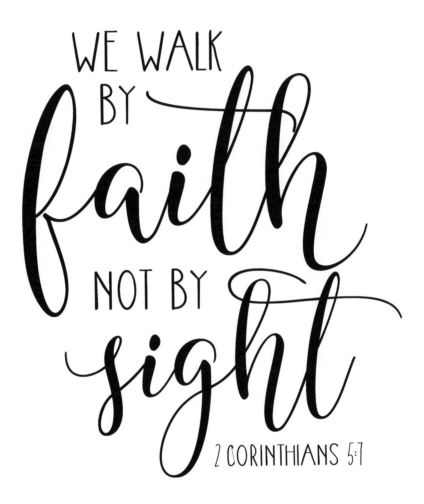

PRACTICE:

PRACTICE:

YOU ARE THE

LIGHT

OF THE

WORLD

MATTHEW 5:14

PRACTICE:

SET YOUR
mind
ON THINGS
above

COLOSSIANS 3:2

PRACTICE:

PRACTICE:

trust
IN THE
Lord
WITH ALL YOUR
heart

PROVERBS 3:5

PRACTICE:

MAY THE LORD BLESS YOU AND KEEP YOU,
MAY THE LORD LIFT HIS FACE TO SHINE UPON YOU,
AND GIVE YOU PEACE.

79157951R00046

Made in the USA
Lexington, KY
18 January 2018